Skin of the Sun
Erick Blue

Copyright © 2021 Erick Blue

All rights reserved. No part of this book may be reproduced or transmitted in any form or by any means, electronic or mechanical, including photocopying, recording or by any information storage and retrieval system without permission in writing from the publisher.

Blue Sky Extra Press—Madison, WI
ISBN: 978-0-578-85169-3
Library of Congress Control Number: 2021907060
Title: *Skin of the Sun*
Author: Erick Blue
Digital distribution | 2021
Paperback | 2021

This is a work of fiction. The characters, names, incidents, places, and dialogue are products of the author's imagination, and are not to be construed as real.

*I recognize no dichotomy between
art and protest.*
—*Ralph Ellison*

*If you living carefree then you probably
don't look like us.*
—*Mick Jenkins*

*If it's meant to be, then it'll be
if it's not, then fuck it, I'ma try
ain't no need to ask the Father why.*
—*J Cole*

Dedication

For the Southside

Table of Contents

History of a Black Body 1
My Skin Be 1 Corinthians 13: 4-8 2
Raindrops and Black Boys Evaporate 4
S.S Raiders 6
Ode to Kobe 8
New Age Horror Films 9
Barber Shop Chronicles (part 1) 11
Silence of Trees 12
(How) Does My Country Love Me? 13
Your System 15
Bury Me Next to Fo' Nem 17
Black American Family Tradition 19
They Murdered Jesus in the Streets Too 20
Barber Shop Chronicles (part 2) 21
Sorrow in These Streets 22
Perfectly Aligned 23
Love for Black Love 24
Haiku for Haku 25
Dat Black Boy Free 26
Moonlight Lullaby 27
Reflection (Been a Long Time Comin') 28
Acknowledgements 31

History of a Black Body

Walk past as if I was never there,
invisible not hiding in camouflage
just me, just another body, nothing

that stands out. Perceived as a white dot
on the pale painted walls of the wealthy.
If I could talk, If I could be heard,

would you believe my story? Wouldn't you
want to trace my words feeling every twist,
loop, and line from this fuchsia tongue?

My story is more than just Malcolm & Martin,
more than the facts you were given reading
from a book.

Books aren't worthy to recite my story!
For the glory of it survives in my heart
spewing from my mouth but with no one to listen.

Walk past like I was never there,
ignoring this difference we share
for your comfort

not knowing the treasure you'll hold once you
step out that zone. See me in this darkness
my light will illuminate, so

pour more if you need
no liquid can take out the flame
it's all gasoline.

My Skin Be
1 Corinthians 13: 4-8

My skin be
    patient,
My skin be
    kind,
My skin be
    not envious,
My skin be
    not boasting,
My skin be
    not self-seeking,
My skin be
    not easily angered,
My skin be
    rejoicing in truth,
My skin be
    always protecting,
My skin be
    always hoping,
My skin be
    unfailing,
My skin be
    passing knowledge,
My skin be
    truthful,
My skin be
    trustworthy,

My skin be
 hopeful,
My skin be
 persevering.

Raindrops and Black Boys Evaporate

I feel you
thirsty,
parched,
way before you can feel me
permit me to cleanse the weary parts of
you. Traveling through the deserts of strain
& tension creates mirages comforting but
apocryphal to reality. Tilt your head back
as I run down your face trailblazing my own
path trickling through your dirt patched face
skin of the sun, cooling your temperature to satisfaction.

Although this care may seem
complete,
that isn't my
goal.

A lone drop, falling from glory I am
you and I are similar
wanting to be caught mid air but
rock bottom is inevitable.
Wanting to lay there, staring at the twinkle gleaming from
another galaxy
dreaming of evaporation to bring me closer the glow
**removed from the nimbus cloud, yearning for that one of a kind
snowflake design yes -**

changing my state of matter, becoming more conscious of my
own science
we are in a puddle of lost hopes, but yet still dream
we dream of rising
the only thing that can make us rise again
are more fallen raindrops.

S.S Raiders

I've never witnessed a mother's fear like the first time her baby boy first runs on that field as a young warrior armed

for war. His armor laced in pearlescent black with hand me down Nike cleats that his size 8 feet squeeze into, worn

down from last year's championship season. I watched as her heart raced, the expression of trepidation displayed

through her body, so stiff & still as her hands protect her mouth from screams of terror yes, this was a different fear.

Similar to the fear mothers have of sending their sons to the Seven Eleven, anticipating on their return but the security of

their return causes high concern, so as he is gone mom watches the local news to hear of any incidents. She watches her baby

boy in the huddle with his team of warriors and can hear sacred southside chants that serenade opponents ears like a

siren luring bait. She watches as her baby boy lines up with the rest of his squad with his foe across from him, glaring in

his eyes. I observe rage building in her eyes from the thought of that foe causing any harm to her baby boy. Her eyes cutting into that kids jersey deeper than mariana trench ready to die for hers. The play starts and brown swine skinned ball is

thrown to her baby boy with eyes wider than the field itself. Bracing herself for an impact collision from their enemy, he

catches the oblong object while simultaneously escaping all danger heading his way, sprinting perfectly to the promise

land. Relieved because her baby boy was saved & baptized, washed in the precious blood of Jesus.

Ode to Kobe

Kobe 8 to 24 LA's greatest we miss you big facts,
high school carried the 33 like Kareem on his back
Had the dream like Hakeem & kept LA on the map,
you would have had ten titles if Wade ain't grabbed Shaq.

Can't complain about five, I know you was chasing the goat,
you were my generations version of him resembling every last stroke
roll or dunk, jumping higher than the clouds & scoring at will,
81 on the Raptors, treating my Suns like your kids all with immaculate skill.

I'll forever cherish your game, mamba mentality put us all in the zone,
from wood boards to cement pavement to dirt roads galore
when the stress builds & emotions grow or I'm feeling alone,
that first bounce of the sphere made my heart feel at home.

I could never thank you enough, I would need 33,643 tongues,
you gave your heart to the game, the net swishing is like melody sung
forever remaining in our hearts a real G.O.A.T & pure artiste,
definition of a true life champion, your legacy lives while you're at peace.

New Age Horror Films

I have watched all of the major slasher series of the 80's & 90's, such as "Halloween", "Friday the 13th", "Child's Play", "Scream", & the great "Stephen King's Children of the Corn". I have watched the gore and blood splatter caused by these fictional creatures committing heinous acts upon those that cross their paths. They have become so predictable that I can foresee when the damsel is going trip, or when the lead white guy solely decides that the group is going to split up, leaving the black folks (if they are still alive) to fend for themselves. The fictitious entertainment these films hold allow them to be bearable to its viewers because it is just that, fiction.

True fear comes from watching "When They See Us", "Fruitvale Station", "Cash for Kids", "Black Venus", "Just Mercy", "Boyz in the Hood", "Clemency", "Get Out", "The Hate U Give", "To Kill a Mockingbird"... these are my horror films. I view myself as the protagonist of these stories, like a biography I've never lived. I watch as characters are emotionally slaughtered way past the point of reconciliation while being physically

broken only to be left standing on death's doormat. These tales of the
justice system & black bodies have become the new age horror films,
authentic terror.

Barber Shop Chronicles (part 1)

Palm on palm, now the back side. The motion of a formal black greeting with 90's r&b soothing my ears. The old heads saying to me, *what you know about this youngblood?* I shake my head even though I've heard these same lyrics every Saturday morning while mama stress cleaned, or when pops didn't come back home the night before. Noise all drowns out once I sit in the chair & the buzzing of the clippers begins to take away the rough edges, chiseling me like a marble statue, into
a masterpiece.
This crisp lining & taper fade got me looking like the first day of school. These twisted curls float & bounce as if my hair touched the exosphere, defying gravity. No physics equation or any mathematical algorithms can solve this phenomenon. An old head says to me, *I used to have that hairstyle before I went to war.* Not anywhere overseas but, the domestic war over streets to claim Fisher & Beld,
the blood still flows through Penn Park. Before I rise off the throne, the old me is swept away clearing way for my state-of-the-art look. My barber mixes the alcohol with water like a Pearlee's Thursday night to take away some of the sting, but I prefer it. The pain reminds me of what I had endured
to wear this crown.

Silence of Trees

Lonesome,
branches stretch wide reaching
but touch nothing.
It's as if the wooden limbs are decaying
succumb to an illness no other tree wants.
Termites.
It's roots deep
6 ft deep
death's door is only a knock away.
Ask the tree who hears it when it cries
not the chainsaw from the grip of
bearded men displayed in denim & plaid
nor the woodpecker consuming the disease
away like a white blood cell.
It is the other trees also reaching out
their branches & yet receive no touch
the lonely tree yearns to be heard
when it falls.
Nothing can explain its sincere silence.

(How) Does My Country Love Me

DON'T kneel.
Respect the flag.
Be grateful.
FORGET the past.
I'm constantly reminded to love my country
to uphold ITS standards to be an "American".

Don't forget...

Don't forget...

Does my country love me as I look in my rear view lens & see those primary colors? As I'm stuck
wide eyed
lacking oxygen
thinking why I didn't tell my mother I loved her
before I left her house?

Does my country love me when a moonlit sky as dark as ebony overcast itself? I'm counting the steps I'm allowed to take before I look like trouble.

Does my country love me when the just unjustly
take life, after life, after life, after life, after life, after life, after life, after life, after life, after life, after life, after life, after life, after life, after life, after life, after life, after life, after

life, after life, after life, after life, after life, after life, after life,
after life, after life, after life, after life, just
destroying families?
A son, a mother, a daughter, a father, sister, brother
remembered by a shirt and hashtag.

Does my country love me
when I pay tuition just like you, yet you are annoyed by my
achievements?
Security for who, have I lost the right to be here?
Prove to me I don't! The police are on their way,
sirens & lights blaze through the inclusive diversity
poster on the window.

Does my country love my unapologetic hair, my cocoa bean
skin,
my relentless culture which is ridiculed for its naturality,
yet still is appropriated by the masses?

Does my country love me when I have to be five
times as good as you to only earn half of
what you've been given?

    Thee America: the greatest country in the world, you could be
                                                                     next.

                My America: reset everyday, will I be next?

Your System

Why,
do you generalize a collective of humans
put them in a box
bind them together
under ship decks or walls 6ft x 8ft
giving nothing but darkness & spoiled air.
Remembering your ancestors
beat,
burned,
raped,
humiliated
deceived mine yet -
you want me to change
your label?
Claiming your lack of presences cleans the blood off your
hands,
saying get
over
it.
You've given me mine, USDA approved
from the first air I was able to breathe
with the impression that I cannot change it &
through the oppression I have to stand,
toe to toe
face to face
ego to ego
Martin's, mind to mind

Malcom's, fist to fist.
My objection overruled by your generations of
lies & hate & fears
it burns tallies through my skin
a smoky flesh branded like cattle.
Purity left the world after the first bite, but
why should I have to prove my innocence?
Haven't you enough to keep up with?
The sound of your gavel makes my soul ache
knowing I'll never have true liberation
on this side of the Atlantic.
To you
   my skin
      my fate
         my melanin
            makes me
                          guilty.

Guilty, til proven
dead.

Bury Me Next to Fo' Nem

I'm tired, no
I'm tired of being tired.
How my grandma stared at my grandpa tired, with
indignation, wrath, or even vexation
yeah let's go with one of those.
I can't keep feeling like this
every week, every day that
feeling causing you know
stomach drops, shaking my head, teary eyes.
Anger is too easy to describe this pressure from being buried
alive
so much that my mind and soul begins to crystallize as my body
hardens,
a round princess cut.

No, this such feeling has no name
it's a feeling truly unlocked.
A feeling only spoken in Braille, becoming fluent in my
blood by it piercing my heart, ohhhh -
not by the people who eat gelatin & Mexican rice at their local
ponderosa
claiming their palate is cultured,
it's the ones whose ancestors rode the boat like mine.
The constant loss of black bodies to the stripes & stars of a
waving cloth
dictate rules to live by,
not my rules to survive.

You look at the grave & see death
I look and the grave & there's peace,
everything I've ever needed.
The empty tomb that
most would call their last home,
well make sure to call it my mansion!

This is a gated community right?

Can I kick my feet up while singing praises to the Lord?
Rejoice on marble countertops?
Mind where you walk on this gold pavement.

Black American Family Tradition

My niece is 12 years old, my sister is explaining to her about
Breonna Taylor.
When my niece was 7 years old, my sister was explaining to her about
Sandra Bland.
When my sister was 8 years old, my dad was explaining to her about
Rodney King.
When my dad was 5 years old, my grandma was explaining to him about
Emmett Till.
This is a tradition that black Americans practice.
The delicate heirloom.
The generational curse.

They Murdered Jesus in the Streets Too

You see how they do us, or is it just us?
No justice no peace but they always telling us to
know justice, know peace follow Dr. King in the
streets march & sing in these streets. Stand strong
& get beat in these streets. Nah, like Rosa responded
when that white man told her to move. I refuse to stand &
continue to watch my brothers & sisters, aunties, & uncles
get attacked and abused - I just can't go! 400 years in this
country built on our backs while whip scars come from
the arduous sound of cracks and burning brands to tag us
on stolen land. Today, my precious melanin still makes me
a threat because it irritates the white skin like a blackhead
deemed as a blemish in society. Textbooks filled with lies &
false presumptions, not spilling black truth while fueling
minds with destruction - causing more reduction to our
history. Religion weaponized in this genocide only to justify
centuries of your wicked behavior. Portraits of white Jesus
sweep the Earth like a sand storm in the Sahara. Jesus is black!
You can't tell me he isn't. With the geological evidence,
historians, & artifacts it is certain that Jesus is black. He is
a black man like no other yet treated like another. True identity
hidden behind a mask giving false perception of who He is.
Curious to how America would recognize Him?
Do you see Him In Medgar, Stokley, or Huey?
In Maya, Ruby, or Harriet?
In Ahmaud, Treyvon, or George?
Do you see Him in me?

Barber shop Chronicles (part 2)

Back to the shop, back to the throne, back to get my weekly fix of cocoa oil sheen & Cantu conditioner. I know Monique was feeling me last time I caught her eye on the block with this fade. She smirked at me with a tasteful grin when I sauntered by, left me feeling like grandma's sweet potato pie, warm and sweet. I hunger for that same cut that, same shape up with the taper that regard from Monique oh how her eyes carved, her lips curled. It's

a constant replay in my head, over and over of that moment anticipating our next sidewalk union as the clippers buzz & trim away last week's memories and stress. My barber observes the glow in my eye as I am mesmerized by my thoughts, gazing candidly into my reflection. He adds a little more shine on my tapered edges, leaving a chatoyant luster. A deep voice devours my ears penetrating far into my apex, *she only gonna love you til your hair grow back nappy*, & I replied, t*hen I'll be back for my fix.*

Sorrow in these Streets

    God bless the streets;
them same streets that consumed Dre before he could get to his
after school rec center; yeah them same streets that his mother
prayed for while he grew up around the og's from the block.
The street lights were a decree that he didn't abide by so he had
all the father time that mother nature would allow-
chasing his middle school sweetheart
and benjamins.
    At 14 Dre got his first piece,
not from his now high school shorty who was infatuated with
his collections of Jumpman's, blinded by his arrogance.
He copped that gat, cannon, six-shooter, strap declaring his
presence on the front line of any war from an opp.
    Dre's homie got murdered
over his now prom date, she played homie like a flute whistling
in the wind. Silently, the opps got him. Dre lets it be known,
his mind madly dashing & heart cooling to absolute zero,
*You drill mine the blood leaks I cocks nines, uzi's and gats,
more straps, it's revenge time.* These rhymes ingrained in the
concrete, blood flows over the sediment washing away a
mothers tears as she bathes in her childs gore, Dre cast
these spells in these blessed streets.

Perfectly Aligned

I know the difference. The space between
the structure compared to the struggle, there is no resemblance. Only the remembrance of the past. The feelings, they last & hold every time I watch the news. This wasn't supposed to be, but somehow we're meant to be. The universe, the galaxy, is always clear & only puts forth its designed masterpiece. Any blemish, it won't last. Nah, time will wind out dismantling anything that isn't
pure, cleansing our souls daily for the enlightenment of Him. So His light can shine through me; through us. Truly I

put my trust in Him
put my trust in Him

to see us through, even when the fog is heavy & our words won't let us subdue ourselves. Creating new storms in our atmosphere, yes, to seek that dazed feeling nothing quite like it. Gets me through the long dark nights.

Love for Black Love

Ebony. Raven. Sable. Onyx.
Charcoal. Jet. Black.

Let me pour into you running your cup to the brim,
cherishing the missing devotion you rightfully deserve.

Infatuated by your midnight glow & the novels
held by your deep, thick roots. This love heals

the underlying pains the world only known by ebony. Just a
touch of this love restores spirits & rejuvenates prosperity.

Black woman are secure & protected
Black men are alive & present
Black love is born by a different light

created not to shine only in darkness
but purely created to shine, period.

Haiku for Haku

What a blessing it
      is to be chosen for you
kind, devine, black prince.

Dat Black Boy Free

They say dat black boy got joy, that dat black boy is jovial
that black boy aint got a care in the world. I watch dat black boy
grasping greatness without extending a limb. He sits there with
his notepad & favorite colored pencils examining every detail
tracing every line that curves or coils. Combat contest between
Sasuke, Inuyasha, and Almight in the nihon teien that the pad sheet
holds. Transferring worlds to be amongst celestial bodies, using the
cosmos as his playground. I am left on this same sphere deprived
of such dark matter that dat black boy emmenates. I envy his freedom,
his sovereignty, his exemption for I am shackled like owned property
reduced by fast whips & gold chains. I say, dat black boy free
because he knows the true nature of peace.

Moonlight Lullaby

S P A C E
In the clustered abyss
eyes penetrate those surface wounds
of maria & terrae
scarred and desperate
blue in the face
representing the night sky
simultaneously lonely yet,
significant.

Plainly,
gleaming down
to light the way
that gold radiance
primary, only to understand
reveal the way
glow, shine.

I lay next to my shadow
black through darkness
drowning in comfort and peace
a battery recharge for what waits,
energy exhausted from today
sleep now.

Reflection (Been a long time comin')

This one gotta be personal between you and you, not one that makes you perceive a false reality of what life could of been but what life actually is. Look into that glass speculum with deep admiration penetrate into yourself, that image which once was callous and dense, rigid in unruly places now tender, clear, and easy. Smooth and straight from what once was twisted. The progression of thought and decision, growth and development of the frontal lobe that doesn't burden the heart of mothering souls who can observe you becoming what they always thought of you. What you thought of you. You are constructed from every mistake you have ever made. Behold the beauty in the struggle from which you came, leaving the results even more exquisite and wonderful in every insignificant detail. Been a long time comin'.

About the Author

Erick Blue is a born and bred product of Madison, Wisconsin's South Side. By day Erick is an educator for the Madison Metropolitan School District specializing in Behavioral Education. In his off time, Erick continues to give back to his community through his artistry - writing poetry, painting, making music and being an advocate for social justice. Erick is a trailblazer, a role model, a visionary and most importantly, a Black man who strives to make Madison a more inclusive place for all. Skin of the Sun is his first published work, but stay tuned - he's not finished yet.

Acknowledgements

God, for life, I'm grateful for everything You've done, are doing, & are going to do. Your love is eternal. Everything I am is from You.

Mom, Grandma, Auntee, the pillars in my life, the true strength behind the family.

Richard Jones & Marcus Porter, my brothers. My fellow creators. My fellow artist. Thank you for the valuable time spent editing and critiquing this body of work with me. Thank you for believing in me.

Ciara Nash, thank you for sharing your art, creating beautiful illustrations helping to make *Skin of the Sun* possible.

Rob Dz, thank you for showing me how to express myself at a young age. You've always believed in the black kids in Madison.

Clint Smith, Denez Smith, Mahogany Browne, Hanif Abdurraqib, thank you for providing countless hours reading & reflecting on your art while falling in love, reciting & connecting with your words.

Matthew Guenette, thank you for helping me discover my interest in writing & and being a guide towards using it as an art.

Em Hughes, thank you for believing in this book & giving it a chance to touch and connect to readers.

To those fallen to police brutality & white supremacy, you will never be forgotten for your legacy lives with us. To the Madison youth, thank you for the hope you bring towards being the change the world desperately needs.

Thank You

www.ingramcontent.com/pod-product-compliance
Lightning Source LLC
Chambersburg PA
CBHW021413290426
44108CB00010B/516